Haunted Inns

of the Chilterns
& Thames Valley

by
ROGER LONG

Photographs: Brenda Allaway
Artwork: Chris Hart

W
WOODFIELD
FONTWELL · SUSSEX · ENGLAND

First published in 1993 by
Woodfield Publishing
Woodfield House, Arundel Road
Fontwell, Arundel, West Sussex, UK

© Roger Long, 1993

A Catalogue Record of this title
is held at the British Library

ISBN 1 873203 23 3

Printed in England

Contents

Foreword

I count myself as arguably the nation's number one pub crawler. I started quite illegally at the tender age of 15, as my friends and I slipped off our tell-tale school blazers and ties and surreptitiously visited numerous pubs in the area. By the time I had reached the legal drinking age of 18, I had a list of over 1,000 pubs that I had conned a drink from.

I kept this list for a number of years and, by the age of 36, I had reams of it with the names, addresses and descriptions of over 14,000 hostelries I had visited both at home and abroad. These featured 34 separate calls in Aberystwyth in one day, 38 in Margate in another, and an all time crowning achievement of 50 in York!

Unfortunately, in the following year, whilst moving house, this unique list disappeared. The loss of my life's work distressed and depressed me greatly. As a loss to humanity it must rank in importance with the Turin Shroud, the Dead Sea Scrolls or the originals of Shakespeare. There was no going back, many of the pubs had been demolished or had changed their function in life. Not only that but the cost of travelling alone would have been astronomical, so this document will remain a most lamented part of my past.

From the age of 36–46 (my present age) I have compiled various lists that amount to some 4,000 different hostelries in the last ten years. I have been in the transport business most of my life and it was so easy to pull up at various towns for the night and stroll around 10 or 12 different pubs or inns.

The second list pales into insignificance compared to the original, and I deem it of no value whatsoever.

For readers wondering if I'll ever come to the point of this boastful and much elaborated account of my mis-spent youth, it is as follows: if one were to compute the complete total of different inns I have visited, one comes up with an approximate total of 18,000. Unbelievable perhaps, but I assure you it is an absolute fact. If one were then to add the literally thousands of visits I have made to some two dozen hostelries that I class as locals, one comes up with an astronomical figure in excess of 25,000.

If the theory of probability exists then one would imagine the chances of encountering inexplicable phenomena to be very high considering that pubs in general have a reputation for such phenomena. Not so. In nearly thirty years of meandering in pubs, inns and hotels at the rate mentioned above, in various stages of sobriety I have come across only one experience that I found inexplicable (in the morning that is). This experience, being well outside the geographical extremes of this book, namely in upper Gloucestershire, I shall not inflict an account upon the reader.

The point I hope I have finally made, is that you could travel around the 45 hostelries listed in this book for a number of years without experiencing anything supernatural whatsoever. However, you would not get very far without finding some local who would convincingly state that he or a close friend or relative had witnessed something weird and supernatural.

I myself approach every tale with an open mind, even with an outlook verging on the sceptical. Hence the *reputedly* haunted pubs of the Thames Valley and Chilterns.

·PART ONE·

The Eastern Thames Valley

WARFIELD

The Plough and Harrow

Warfield is a large but sparsely populated village, some three miles North of overpowering and modernised Bracknell. It is more of a collection of small hamlets than a village, strung together by narrow and winding roads.

At a crossroads where the road from Bracknell meets the Forest Road, stands the Plough and Harrow, in what could arguably be described as the centre of the village.

The pub itself neither possesses nor claims any spiritual activity. The offending venue is the car park and the Forest Road that passes the old inn's door.

The story is a rather colourful one. Warfield Park, now demolished, was a large and pleasant house about a mile south of the Plough and Harrow. In the 1870's it was owned and dominated by Lord Ormanthwaite and his wife Lady Emily, daughter to the Duke of Beaufort. The Lady was a local philanthropist, bestowing goods and doing charitable work for the community. This made her very popula. Her husband however, was supposedly a man with a quick temper and a violent nature.

When it came to the ears of the local populace that Lord Ormanthwaite had been particularly violent towards his long-suffering Lady, the villagers decided to give him a taste of what is known locally as "canning". It involved a large party of villagers (some reports say four hundred, but this is probably a gross exaggeration) obtaining anything that made a loud noise, i.e. cooking utensils, pots, pans and the like, whistles, pipes and spades, and marching, late at night to Warfield Park, and there making the most horrific din, thereby demonstrating their justifiable umbrage to their Lord.

Lord Ormanthwaite retaliated by taking the names of some of the ringleaders concerned and later charging them with unlawful assembly.

These events took place on October 28th 1874, and it is said that on that date every year, a spectral ragged band is heard travelling down the forest road to the Plough and Harrow, there to meet with others from the North of the village near the church. The combined forces make their way across the fields in the direction of Warfield Park.

In 1974 on the one hundredth anniversary of the event a local paper reported this story at some length. The result was that several intrepid ghost hunters spent the night camping in the vicinity of Forest Road in the vain hope of experiencing this phenomenon. Needless to say they were disappointed.

An old chap I once knew in Warfield claimed to have first hand knowledge of the event, even to the extent of stating that his father was one of the original marchers. Later, by checking dates, I ascertained that this was chronologically possible. He definitely told a very convincing story. He mentioned about a

crippled boy in the village with a badly clubbed foot, whose only desire in life was to become a soldier. His deformity obviously would stop him from achieving this ambition. The Lady Emily, knowing of the boy's plight, had him tailored a bright red tunic of military style, and also provided him with a drum. These were his favourite possessions other than a pet monkey, a present from a recently demised soldiering father.

The spirit of the drummer boy, with his constant companion the monkey, is said to lead the throng with a measured tread as they approach Warfield Park. The story sounds plausible. I don't think the drummer was a figment of my informer's imagination. After all, aged villagers have since informed me that there was once a pub in Warfield called the "Drum and Monkey". Possibly named in honour of our limping young hero. Who knows?

WARFIELD

The Tudor Rose

Literally a stone's throw away from the Plough and Harrow, in fact almost adjacent stands the Tudor Rose. Ancient as the building is, it has been a bar and restaurant for less than a decade. I believe the licence was granted in the early 1980's. Prior to this it was a tea room patronised by the more affluent and discerning inhabitants of the village (the tea-cake, cucumber sandwich and scone brigade).

When the owner finally put the old place up for auction she informed *The Bracknell News* about its resident shdowy apparition . . . The owner stated that, old as the building was (some two hundred and fifty years), it was built on the site of a far more ancient dwelling, the original building being a staging post, where monks provided rest and sustenance for travellers who braved the wild courseways of Windsor Forest. This supposition is in no small way borne out by the profusion of monastic place names in the area, indeed there is a 'Priory Lane' less than a hundred yards from the building.

It is therefore not surprising that the ghostly figure which was often glimpsed in the old tea rooms was a cowled figure dressed in black. I use the word 'glimpsed' in the past tense, for the unknown brother has not appeared for some twenty-five years. This is not to say that he hasn't made his presence felt. The odd paper pot and plate have been known to develop a will of their own in far more recent times, and as recently as ten years ago a low almost inaudible chanting was detected. Obviously the gentleman was not from an order that observed a vow of silence.

Several ladies who have worked in the establishment have felt an atmosphere created by some sort of presence. But the feeling is described as a benign rather than malicious experience.

The Herne's Oak

ust along the Forest Road from Warfield in an Easterly direction lies the village of Winkfield. It is more than a sister to Warfield, it is a twin sister. Again we have a village that is very widespread and thinly populated. The two are so similar it is difficult to establish just exactly where the dividing line is.

The Herne's Oak has very little claim to psychic phenomena but it was rumoured that in the 1940's, the sound of unshod galloping hooves was heard outside. If the supernatural involvement of the Inn itself is tenacious and less well authenticated, the ghostly spectre that it commemorates is certainly not.

The case of 'Herne the Spectral Hunter' has probably appeared in more supernatural anthologies than any other, with the possible exception of Ann Boleyn. Speculation has been rife for centuries and various stories have been advanced from all manner of writers. It is because of these varied and colourful ruminations, and its slender association with the pub of that name, that I have justified my reason, nay excuse, for its inclusion here.

Herne is probably as old as time itself. He is likely to be of paleolithic origin and may have something to do with fertility ceremonies. For years people in this country have worshipped such pagan gods. The green man that adorns so many pub signs is depicted covered in foliage, often with the antlers of a deer on his head and a flaming torch in his hand.

Ceremonies in all parts of the country include horn dances, where men wear antlers and dance holding maidens and leading hobby horses. A prime example is at Abbots Bromley in Staffordshire where the traditional merrymaking takes place early in September.

The wearing of animal heads became synonymous with black magic and witchcraft. Even today, werewolves are still associated with a similar appearance. In the 7th century, Theodore, Archbishop of Canterbury, publicly condemned any man caught masquerading as a beast, proclaiming it to be devilish beyond belief.

There is also a strong school of thought that associates Herne with the Norse god Odin or Woden, that the fire breathing horse is Sleipher (Odin's favourite mount) and that the baying hellhounds are Cain's Pack. Also the shrieking gigantic owl that sits upon Herne's shoulder is Turtsel, again famous in Norse mythology.

Another somewhat tenuous explanation links Herne with Cernunnes, the Celtic god of the underworld.

If we leap forward to the late 14th century we find Herne employed as a forester by Richard II, a favourite of this king of violence and arbiter of nature, but having been gored badly by a stag the woodsman fell from favour as he had lost his inbuilt sense for finding game. Blaming himself for his shortcomings, he brooded deeply in his home in the forest. Finally his brain gave way and he hanged himself from what was to become the famous Herne's Oak.

Later stories deny that Herne was Richard's forester and place him as the gamekeeper and huntmaster of Henry VIII. His expertise in hunting is again mentioned and was very much appreciated by the egotistical Henry. This was greatly to the annoyance of other hunters who inferred to the king that such an uncanny ability could only be the outcome of witchcraft. Herne overheard this and rather than go through the excruciating tortures of the time, hanged himself on the large oak tree near his hovel in the forest.

As you can see, the stories bear a striking similarity.

Yet a third version of the same story places Herne as a warden of the forest, for Elizabeth I, with the same untimely ending on an oak tree after being terrified of the good Queen's wrath for committing some trivial offence.

It is hardly likely that the infamous hunter did originate in Elizabethan times, for Shakespeare mentions him as an old legend in the *Merry Wives of Windsor*. Mrs. Ford describes him and some of his deeds such as blasting out trees and putting blood into cows' milk. The motley ladies persuade Falstaff to impersonate Herne for a clandestine assignation with one of them in the forest. One would have thought the obese bulk of Falstaff would have been a severe load for any horse, supernatural or not.

Herne would have held little rapport with anyone of Royalty because a side issue of his haunting is that it foretells the imminent death of the monarch, thus far the prediction would seem to be unfounded. Queen Victoria however placed much credence in the appearance of the huntsman being an ill omen. Perhaps the most graphic description of the spectral huntsman and the most intriguing if unbelievable story comes from Harrison Ainsworth, the Victorian novelist.

The novelist puts Herne undoubtedly in the reign of Richard II. Herne has become the king's favourite because of his skill at hunting. As they were returning home one evening, a wounded stag turned and attacked Richard, Herne jumped straight to his master's defence and after a ferocious battle, managed to stab the stag to death with his dagger.

Herne was seriously injured in the affray and close to death. As the king leaned over his loyal huntsman a stranger mysteriously appeared and told Richard he would save Herne's life.

On the stranger's instructions the other huntsmen bound the stag's antlers to Herne's head and then carried him to the stranger's lonely hut on Bagshot Heath, there to be tended until his recovery, whereupon the king would enrich him for his bravery and loyalty.

The other huntsmen, on reaching the stranger's hut and seething with jealousy, threatened the mysterious man with death should he let the hunter recover. The man replied that he could not break his word to his sovereign, but he would make sure that Herne would never again be popular with the king. If he did this, he warned them that they would risk the wrath of Herne for the rest of their lives. A bargain was struck.

When Herne finally recovered, he was without a sense of smell or hearing and all his woodland knowledge had gone. In this state he was no use to the impatient king who ungratefully threw him out of his job and home. As in the other stories, Herne walked dejectedly deep into the forest and hanged himself from the great oak tree.

His body was discovered by one of the conspirators who quickly ran to find the others. By the time he returned, the body was gone.

Herne's curse soon began to take effect. The deer seemed to have fled the whole forest, horses fell ill from unknown ailments. The impatient king was as angry with the huntsmen as he had been with Herne. In desperation they sought out the stranger, but he gave them little solace; he said they must placate the spirit of Herne that resided in the great oak tree.

At midnight on the following night the huntsmen were gathered at the tree when the stranger appeared in a wisp of smoke, accompanied by the spectral Herne complete with horse, baying hounds and antlers. Earthbound and spectral huntsmen hunted until dawn slaying all that were left of the king's prize deer.

On hearing the news, Richard and the stranger cautiously approached Herne's Oak. The mystical hunter's spirit appeared and informed the king that if the hunters who had brought about his downfall were punished, he would have no more forays whilst the king lived.

The huntsmen were executed, the deer returned and Herne kept his word, at least while Richard II lived.

The history and whereabouts of the particular oak Herne haunted is as variable and speculative as the story of Herne himself. The great oak was reputed to be about half a mile south of Windsor in the Home Park area. The original was destroyed in 1796 by mistake, although George III vehemently denied this. It was re-planted in Victorian times apparently this time on the wrong site. It was destroyed again in 1896. Whether this was the one on the incorrect site or not is not clear.

Several books refer to yet another Herne's Oak being destroyed in 1906. Even others refer to the stump of the original oak still being visible on a footpath in the vicinity of Queen Adelaide's lodge in Little Park.

An unusual and terrifying encounter with the phantom hunter was experienced by no lesser a personage than the Earl of Surrey. He had been warned not to ride near the dreaded oak but had ignored the warning. Suddenly he was blinded by a blue phosphoric light streaming down on him from the branches. This initial shock was followed by a drumming of hooves and then a creature, half man and half beast, covered in animal skin, screamed across the clearing on horseback. The Earl described it as the most uncanny and terrifying sight of his life.

On a later occasion, the Duke of Richmond was sheltering in the forest and saw the whole spectral hunt from some way off. He described the blowing of the horn and a succession of phantom hounds and huntsmen led by the demonical Herne himself.

It was obvious that in the 17th and 18th centuries, highwaymen and footpads exaggerated and expounded the haunting to keep a gullible, but curious, peasantry at home and away from their nocturnal exploits.

Sightings over the years have virtually died out. Early this century, two Eton schoolboys reported witnessing something, but their reports would seem to have been enigmatic to say the least. Other sightings of Herne have been of a spasmodic nature, and some obviously being of flippant intention. In 1979 there was a quite well attested one, but even this smacked of deliberate hoax. I believe the unfortunate spectral huntsman was self exorcised many years ago.

WINDSOR

Sir Christopher Wren's House Hotel

Four miles through the Great Park from Winkfield lies Windsor itself, a town steeped in majesty and antiquity. Surely, one would think, a veritable mecca for the spirit world. Old houses, shops and inns abound. Cobbled and narrow streets meander between prestigious and romantic Victorian Georgian and Edwardian veneers. Surely this is fertile soil for the mysterious. A cornucopia of enticing secret enigma.

On the surface one would be correct. There is no shortage of tales of haunting and the inexplicable. The Castle itself boasts at least four royal shades – Henry VIII, Elizabeth I, Charles I and poor mad George III. They rub shoulders with people as socially varied as the Duke of Buckingham and a weeping groom.

The Great Park also seems to be well catered for. There is the already much publicised Herne as well as a ghostly white hart, a terrible disfigured man and a guardsman that patrols the long walk. Back in town there are supposedly haunted houses in Park Street, Sheet Street, Peascod Street and Thames Street to name but a few. However, it would seem that although spooks abound in Windsor, the vast majority of them have taken the pledge. The play on words is that *the old town has a plethora of teetotal spirits*, a point borne out by first hand experience. After enquiring in some thirty or more of the oldest pubs in town. I can only trace one that has any history of the supernatural whatsoever.

The Sir Christopher Wren's House Hotel is at the bottom of Thames Street facing the water. It is a very attractive building indeed and its setting is superb. There is much conjecture amongst experts in town as to whether or not Wren built, or even ever lived in, the building. Be that as it may, for years it was suspected of being cursed.

In its early days the house was owned by a family named Cheshire. They were certainly a very unlucky family if rumour is to be believed. Several members suffered from weird illnesses indigenous to foreign countries in which they had never travelled. One of the daughters had an illegitimate child and a breakdown in that order. The bastard child died in infancy but its mother never got over it. She never came out except in the very late or very early hours. Mr Cheshire nearly died of food poisoning, the less charitable at the time suggesting it was administered by his lamenting daughter. Shortly after this his finances forced him to move into a smaller house – in all possibility a blessing in disguise. Another daughter's engagement was broken off at the last minute. She was betrothed

to a peer of the realm who suddenly deemed the match unsuitable. Could you blame him? Few young men would be enticed by a marriage to a lady whose sister was unbalanced and promiscuous, whose father nearly died of food poisoning and whose family fortune had just gone *up the Swanee*.

It would seem, however, that the curse was definitely on the house and not the family for a stream of owners and tenants came and left in rapid succession over the following hundred years.

In the early 1900s Wren's Old House was acquired by Baroness Vaux who used it for the summer months only. After a few weeks the poor woman was left with a vast mansion and no staff. Serving maids as a breed are known to be imaginative but not to the point of losing their employment. Baroness Vaux could find no servants that would stay. All found the atmosphere in certain parts of the house unbearably malevolent. When the Baroness finally left is not recorded, but after her departure the house remained empty for more than a decade.

For the final part of the story I am indebted to Angus MacNaghten in his *Windsor Hauntings*: apparently the old house was bought by two spinster sisters named Outlaw, turning it first into a tea shop and then an hotel. Since then various consortiums have owned the hotel and internal alterations seem to have subdued the oppressive spirit.

The Cockpit

O ver the bridge from Windsor is the 15th century Cockpit Restaurant and Bar at Eton. It is a picturesque old building set amongst many of such ilk. Now a favourite of Etonians, debs and business executives, it was once, as the name suggests, the scene of barbaric cock fights. The original cockpit – to be found behind the restaurant – is one of the few remaining in England.

It is not difficult to imagine the shouting and anarchy as ribald men hollered to their favourite fighting cock to claw to death its opponent.

Strangely enough, however, the Cockpit's phantom has nothing to do with the cruel and violent scenes once enacted outside. On the contrary, it is a small and apologetic lady who has been seen in the house and occasionally flitting between the tables in the restaurant. Possibly a past owner or long time serving waitress, her manner is unobtrusive and she tries desperately not to give offence.

Previous owners over the years have obviously decided that as no offence seems to be intended, none should be taken. There has been no attempt at exorcism.

Waterman's Arms

N ear to the Thames is the attractive Waterman's Arms. Its beer garden is a must in summer and its is interior intimate and warming at any time of the year. The benevolent and cheery feeling, however, was not always so apparent.

In 1665 the Great Plague was reaping its way through London and stabbing deep into several nearby provincial towns. Windsor was affected and the Waterman's Arms was commandeered as a local mortuary. Could the rumblings and sighing noises heard coming from the cellars over the years be anything to do with the tormented souls of the pestilence's victims?

DATCHET

Royal Stag

There are several parallel roads running from Windsor and Eton to the scenic village of Datchet. The Royal Stag stands on the stately green. It has a very strange tale indeed to relate.

Legend states that some years ago a labourer dropped in for a drink on his way home from work. It was mid-winter and the picturesque village was adorned with snow. The man left his small son outside whilst he stopped to slake his thirst and pass a convivial half hour with other work men. As we know, good company is hard to leave, especially when ale is lubricating conversation. Time passed quickly in such an hospitable atmosphere. Before he realised, the man was late and had completely forgotten about his young son outside.

Time had not passed quickly for the lad. After the general frolics that children indulge in with the snow, the lad had become wet and cold. He had knocked in vain upon the Inn's window with the intention of attracting the attention of his hapless father. This failing, he had tried to enter a nearby church. His lifeless, frozen body was found in a snowdrift against the church wall.

The spectral hand print that periodically appears at the Inn's window is said to be a manifestation of the child's futile plea for help.

Photographs of the appearance of the young boy's hand have been carefully scrutinised over the years and in 1979 the pane of glass was removed to be examined by a London newspaper. Mysteriously the print disappeared from the original pane only to manifest itself on the new one that replaced it.

Jeff Nicholls, an enthusiastic amateur ghost hunter, took some well outlined photographs in April 1984 and reproduced them in the booklet "Our Mysterious Shire". The Landlord had phoned Jeff when the images appeared and he had hurried over post haste to capture them on film.

As a side issue of this story, it has been reported that when a photograph of the boy's handprint was left in the bar overnight, many glasses and bottles were found broken in the morning.

The Royal Stag has experienced any number of strange goings on in addition to the sad shade of the unfortunate labourer's boy. In 1966 William Herbert's gravestone was discovered in the cellar and rumour had it that if it was removed it would be returned by the ghost of the old man himself (quite a feat, one might think, for a spirit, considering the weight of the object!).

There is also a story at the old inn that a room is haunted by something heavy and oppressive that pushes down on the occupant of the bed.

Finally there is a story told to Mr Nicholls by the staff about a toilet that flushes itself. It was the uncanny experience of the landlord's babysitter. She took little notice at first, thinking it to be one of her charges having a game with her. So to make sure there was no chicanery she stood over them. Within a minute it had happened again. Most disconcerting!

The Ostrich

our or five miles east of Datchet the Ostrich Inn still stands in the ancient village of Colnbrook near Slough. The village, now encircled by a by-pass, was once on the main A4, and prior to this, the principal London to Bath stage route.

There is little doubt that there has been some sort of hostelry on the site since the middle ages. The name Ostrich is in all probability a corruption of *hospice*. It has records going back to the reign of Henry II in about 1165. The situation of the old inn made it convenient to wealthy friends of Royalty for changing their clothes before presenting themselves to the Monarch at Windsor. No doubt mud bespattered clothes were substituted for the finery that one adorned oneself in for an audience with the King.

The Ostrich first came to fame, or rather notoriety, through the nefarious exploits of its one time landlord named Jarman. It is a little difficult to put a specific date on when Jarman became "mine host" at the ancient hostelry; the time frame allowed for his villainous actions is flexible indeed. We know that he obviously came after the date of the inn's foundation in 1106, and that he was long gone before the rebuilding around 1500, but other than these two extremes, anything is a matter for conjecture.

Thomas Deloney, reckoned to be England's first novelist, mentions the dastardly goings on in a book in the late 1500's, so the Ostrich has the distinction of being one of the half dozen which claim to be the oldest inn in England, and also definitely being the first one mentioned in an English novel. Deloney's account of the period of Jarman's crimes has many contradictory elements. For instance, he has King Henry I ordering that the inn be burned to the ground in 1130 after Jarman's murders and skulduggery were discovered. We know this did not happen. Thomas Deloney may have used a little poetic licence to embroider a good yarn.

The rather enigmatic facts as far as we know them are as follows: Jarman was the landlord of the Ostrich at some time in the middle ages, probably the 1300s. To supplement his income he devised an intricate and profitable scheme. He would ply a wealthy traveller with drink until he was drunk, and then lead the unfortunate traveller up to his best room. When the unsuspecting man was safely ensconced in a deep slumber, Jarman would pull two bolts from the floor below, and the bed, which was screwed to the floor, would tip at a 45° angle, sliding the poor wayfarer into a great vat of boiling fat that had been strategically placed below. The victim was drowned and boiled to death at the same time. The pain must have been excruciating, but mercifully death was almost instantaneous.

Jarman would then take the man's belongings, deposit the body in a nearby river and sell the man's horse and clothes to the taciturn Gypsies that wandered the moor.

Jarman, it would seem, enjoyed the rewards of his lucrative endeavours for many years. It is not known exactly how he was caught, but there are several theories. One is that the small river or stream was very low one night as it was a particularly dry period. The innkeeper deposited the body as per usual, but by the morning it had not drifted away. It was found by some local horsemen and this was the beginning of the end for Jarman. This theory also suggests that the last unfortunate victim was named Coln, hence the name Colnbrook.

Another theory suggests that an intended victim was at his chamber pot relieving himself after vast quantities of ale, and turned around in time to see his bed at a perilous angle. He ran to the door in his nightshirt, raising the alarm.

Yet another story tells of a young ostler who worked at the inn. The lad heard curses and hollering coming from the kitchen, and on entering the kitchen he discovered the victim feet up in the vat, and Jarman cursing in pain and rubbing spattered fat from his face.

It will never be known how Jarman was caught, but caught he finally was, and condemned to hang. Hanging would seem to be quite a lenient sentence considering the enormity of the crime in those harsh old days. On the scaffold an unrepentant Jarman boasted of some sixty or seventy murders. He no doubt thought "If you've to go, go in style". A nearer estimate of the number of his number of victims would be between fifteen and twenty. As one could be executed for stealing a sheep in those days, the numbers are purely academic.

Jarman certainly made sure of the Ostrich's place in history. In the 1960's a working model of Jarman's equipment was displayed on the bar.

I first published the above story in April 1989 in a magazine named "Master Detective". It was also published in my first book "Murder in Old Berkshire" in September 1990. In neither case did I mention that there had been any supernatural activity at the inn because it was not appropriate to either publication.

There has, however, been some limited strange phenomena experienced over the years by a succession of landlords and staff. The happenings are very nondescript and tame considering the wealth of notorious tradition attached to the pub. They amount to atmospheres in the most part with a few inexplicable bumpings and rumblings in the night. They are blamed generally on one of Jarman's unfortunate victims, but this is pure speculation. It was all a very long time ago.

HURLEY

Ye Olde Bell

From Datchet via the M4 and M308 by-passing Maidenhead it is a short trip to Hurley. The village is steeped in history and has an atmosphere as old as time itself. If all the reported phenomena were to be believed, the reputation of Hurley would rival Pluckey in Kent, famous as Britain's most haunted village. Most tales, however, would seem to be less than well authenticated. It is a chicken and egg situation. The village is a perfect setting for a good ghost story, so no doubt imagination has been exercised to the full and every ancient building has been bestowed with a host of malevolent spirits.

Just in passing, there is one intriguing yarn that seems to be quite well attested. In 1920 a Colonel Rivers Moore purchased Ladye Place which was part of an ancient priory. The Colonel was an accomplished archaeologist and was led to believe that Lady Editha, the sister of Edward the Confessor was buried there. He excavated in a number of places for Lady Editha's tomb without success, but whilst the digging proceeded all manner of spectral monastic personnel visited the good Colonel.

Included was the spirit of a young Benedictine monk in great distress. He communicated, Lord knows how, that he had stolen some jewellery and thrown it down a well in the hope of retrieving it later. He indicated where to dig. This the Colonel did, excavating four centuries of rubble and finally discovering a small basket of gems at the bottom. What the Colonel did with the gems we are not told. He could hardly return them to their rightful owner.

Ladye Place and the ruined priory remained haunted by visiting monks for a number of years; possibly the Colonel found it hard to kick the habit, if you'll pardon the pun.

What has all this to do with Ye Olde Bell? Well, it is one of half a dozen worthy claimants to being Britain's oldest inn. It is without doubt one of the most attractive. Parts of the building are reputed to go back to the year 1135 but most of the present architecture is no older than 15th or 16th century.

There is quite a lot of evidence that there was once an even older building on the site, probably the guest house of the neighbouring priory. An underground passage that starts at the inn, and is suspected to link up with a similar one in the remains of the priory, would seem to lend credence to this idea.

It is from this tunnel, near to where it initiates at the fireplace of Ye Olde Bell, that whimpering or chanting have been heard. One American who stayed there in the mid-seventies claimed to have heard it on several occasions and described it as a lulling sound that exuded a sense of peace and solace. There have been no reports recently of any spiritual sounds. But Ye Olde Bell these days is extremely busy. Probably any monastic chanting would be drowned by the clatter of cutlery and conversation.

Shoppenhangers Manor Restaurant

Back towards Maidenhead along the 423M, looking to one's left, a large and attractive old building may be seen. Now standing behind the Crest Hotel, it can be reached from the centre of the town or from the A4.

The restaurant gives the impression of a baronial banqueting hall. The building was originally part of a 13th century manor but little of the original is left. However, even the new building is by now old enough to be of architectural and historical interest.

In 1971 the ghostly figure of an old man in grey was noticed by a waiter in the restaurant. The figure was described as having the silently gliding movement which is often associated with supernatural forms or shapes. When the perplexed waiter related his experiences the following morning, he was surprised to find that several other members of the staff had also experienced this apparently harmless spectre. All sightings would seem to have occurred about 2am. This is supposedly the time that an old servant of the Tudor lord who once owned the premises, died after falling downstairs.

Oakley Court Hotel

O n the main Maidenhead to Windsor Road lies the hamlet of Oakley Green, its main feature is a vast mansion house, now the prestigious Oakley Court Hotel.

The Oakley Court is one of a group that is justly proud of its image. This hotel, like the others in the chain, equates luxury with romance and epicurean values with respect and efficiency.

It fronts upon the Thames, its vast green lawns leading down to its personal landing stage. In summer it is serenity itself, but this was not always so.

The Oakley Court Hotel was built as a private mansion in 1858 by Sir Robert Saye, undoubtedly an eccentric as far as

architecture is concerned. The Gothic styled building is verging on the bizarre. The twisted towers overpowering and ominous, the weird gargoyles look down, intimidating creations of an anomalous mind. Catch this building on a misty day or on a stormy night, and it is the archetypical reincarnation of Gothic spine chilling terror.

So much does the architecture lend itself to the horror movie that for twenty years the Hammer Film Company used it for their Dracula and Frankenstein movies. The outlandish exterior cloaked with manufactured mist became the hallmark and cinematic foreword of the company.

The accounts of actual supernatural occurrences are most prolific during the second world war. The government took the old place over and lent it to the French Resistance. It was all very hush hush. But it was difficult to obtain any labour locally. People avoided it like the plague. Those stalwarts that were employed there complained of all manner of psychic phenomena, individual experiences so prolific it would be difficult to tabulate.

Perhaps given the setting, imaginations were a little fertile. Perhaps once again the venue evoked the story. As with God, if ghosts had not existed at Oakley Court, it would have been necessary to invent them.

The mansion was left derelict from the mid-fifties to the mid-seventies, and if the building looked bizarre when populated, it looked positively grotesquely moribund when not. I remember well it was a place one did not go near on one's own. It is nicely summed up in the words of Barry Cornwall, the early Victorian poet, "Vague mystery dwells in such deserted places and fear that has no name has wrought his spell".

It was during this period that a local journalist insisted that several local people had found the atmosphere around the building frighteningly oppressive and so menacingly depressive that they had committed suicide in the Thames. This I deem to be a vastly exaggerated report. But strangely enough, the facts fit. Several people did commit suicide by drowning within sight of Oakley Court in that era. This doesn't necessarily mean that the building was a factor. Truth is not merely the facts. Truth is the correct interpretation of the facts. It could have all easily been coincidence.

However, a friend of mine who lived in a flat just outside the derelict building had a very nasty first hand experience. A young woman came screaming to him one day, calling for help as her six year old boy was drowning in the Thames. He ran to give assistance but found he was too late. The body of the young boy was found entangled in the reeds. My friend, still in his teens, tried artificial resuscitation, but his knowledge was limited and his frustrated actions to no avail. At the ensuing inquest he was surprised to receive severe criticism for not doing more. It is difficult to envisage what else he could have done.

A strange rejoinder to this sad little story is that the young woman had already lost two young children drowned in a domestic bath, a strange coincidence that did not escape the notice of the Sunday press. No accusations were ever actually made.

Oakley Court was turned into an hotel in 1982 and since then there have been no reports of any unnatural phenomena.

The White Hart Inn

Returning along the Windsor to Maidenhead Road, turn left just before the motorway bridge signposted Holyport.

Leaving the Green on the right, carry on until you reach a large and gabled pub on the right.

The White Hart possesses one of the many Grey Ladies in the country. She has been seen on many occasions since the second world war, generally around Christmas time.

Evidence suggests over the years that many have heard her but very few have seen the Grey Lady. She differs from her many sisters in one noticeable way: she appears holding a baby. This in itself is unusual if not unique. There have, as far as we know, been no untimely deaths at the White Hart, certainly none concerning mother and child, so the origination of this rather sad spectre is unknown.

The White Hart has an external as well as an internal phantom. A horse, thought, for some unknown reason, to be Kruger, periodically trots by the inn. Kruger was killed by a fall in 1901. At the time he was racing a steeplechase at nearby Hawthorn Hill. Why his apparition should manifest itself on this particular stretch of road is unknown.

The White Hart concludes a spiritual pub crawl of the Eastern Thames Valley.

· PART TWO ·

The Northern and Eastern Chilterns

CHALFONT ST PETER

The White Hart

Chalfont St Peter and its sister villages, Chalfont St Giles and Little Chalfont, nestle in the foothills of the Chilterns. There is not much of old Chalfont St Peter still standing. Fortunately the portion that remains includes the 14th century White Hart.

Just over a century ago this small and attractive hostelry was run by the eccentric Donald Ross. Mr Ross was an avid musician, the violin was his forte and what he lacked in natural talent, he more than made up for in enthusiasm – much to the annoyance of his customers. There are tales of dry throated locals shouting for thirst quenching ale in the bar whilst the self-announced violinist practised upstairs, ignoring his customers.

The would-be violinist Mr Ross died some forty years ago, but the melody lingers on. Those who have heard it have quipped that it may be in the right bar, but it's definitely in the wrong key. The refrain has been noted in living memory by a number of people, the tortured and teeth-edging, haunted refrain wafting into the bar from the room above.

Recently, and some say mercifully, the amount of traffic passing the White Hart's front door has drowned any mystic music that may have been heard.

The White Hart has another supernatural inhabitant, or rather, sound. It is a case of ghostly footsteps on the stairs. Whether or not they belong to the aforementioned Mr Ross is a matter of conjecture, but the footsteps would seem to be synonymous with a particular time of day, namely 4 a.m.

Also, a landlord in the early 1980's awoke to see three spectral figures standing beside his bed. Two quickly disappeared, the third faded after staring at the landlord for nearly a minute. The time was 4 a.m. It was also at this time that fire alarms at the inn went off accidentally on several occasions. Coincidence perhaps, who knows? But it is unusual to find any sort of supernatural manifestation with punctuality amongst its qualities.

❖ ❖ ❖

The Chequers

even or eight miles North West of Chalfont St Peter lies the ancient market town of Amersham, approached via the A413. Inns abound on either side of an historic main street, but before the main town, one may discover one of the most ancient inns of all, The Chequers.

Built in the 15th century and little altered since, this is a pub of character and charm. However, landlords over the years have found the ghostly moaning and other manifestations a little less than charming. Several have left after their families have found the visitations intolerable.

The disquieted spirit would seem to be that of a man named Auden (some say Osman). Auden was employed to guard a group of 16th century martyrs, six men and a woman. They were lodged in the Chequers the night before being burned at the stake the following day at Rectory Woods about a mile away. Auden had a conscience but stuck to his duty. There was no chance of escape.

After the martyrs' deaths, Auden found that guarding them on their final night on earth weighed so heavily upon his conscience that to this day his spirit returns to the scene bewailing his decision.

There is, however, another story that runs parallel to, if not in conjunction with, the former. One of the martyrs was a man named William Tylsworth, and as often happened on such occasions, a close relative, in this case his daughter, was forced to put a lighted faggot to ignite her father's funeral pyre. Her shade now returns to the inn, bemoaning her action and pleading for forgiveness. A pathetic soul in torment.

Whether the distraught wailing is that of Auden or Tylsworth's daughter, it has been sufficiently alarming to necessitate several exorcisms. The first attempt to subdue the moanings and eject the rarely seen gentleman in a dark cassock or cloak took place in 1953. It seemed to have had little effect as another ceremony was performed in 1964.

Between these two dates a local medium was employed and after initiating some type of seance, the lady claimed that she had indeed contacted a man named Auden who was the gaoler of a number of martyrs.

Things then seemed to have quietened down for some time. Until 1971 when a Scottish barman was surprised to see the shade of a man in a dark cloak attempting to climb the chimney although there was a lighted fire in the grate. Was this once again, I wonder, the melancholy gaoler Auden, posthumously trying to share the fate of his martyred charges?

The Crown

Whilst in Amersham, take a stroll down to the Crown, an attractive hotel in the centre of town. The building has been around since the 1620's. However, when the spectre of the little old grey lady first appeared is not recorded. The apparition is described as a friendly one and restricts her visitations to just two rooms, the curiously named Quacks Room and also one at the opposite end of the hotel.

Whoever the little old lady was, she has a very tidy mind. Whereas she is seldom seen these days, evidence of her existence is more common. Guests' clothes that were left strewn on the bed have been placed in wardrobes. Just occasionally, however, it is the reverse. Things have been taken out of drawers and cupboards as if to be inspected. Obviously an inquisitive spectre. Speculation suggests she was once a hotel maid who had nowhere else to live and after her demise just naturally carried on doing her duty in the specific bedrooms alloted to her during her working life.

The White Hart

ld hostelries can still be found in the modern, clinically clean and gleaming, glass and steel clad town of Hemel Hempstead. The antiquated area that remains is slightly to the west of the new town. At the foot of its ancient High Street stands the White Hart.

In the 1850's, when life in the armed services was not popular, the navy employed press gangs to enlist its new recruits. A young man would be plied with strong liquor until he was legless. He would then be thrown upon a cart with several others, also in the same state of inebriation. Occasionally a tap on the head with a cudgel was employed to induce a state of more docile compliance. The unfortunates were later transported to a ship that was due to leave harbour the following morning, to awaken sore headed, some distance from land, to the discovery that they had joined Her Majesty's Navy. Press ganging was popular around most of our coastal towns.

The army were only slightly more subtle, as a young local at the White Hart found to his dismay. The youth had been generously lubricated with strong ale by a couple of gentlemen that he took to be farmers. As he was downing yet another ale from his pewter mug, he felt something smooth and hard nudge his teeth. Depositing it into his hand, he found it to be the Queen's shilling. He had fallen for the oldest trick in the book.

As he turned to his new comrades he noticed that both had shed their top coats and stood there in scarlet tunics. The youth was solemnly informed that he had accepted the shilling, a trooper's first week's pay, and that by doing so he had made a legally binding contract to serve in the Queen's Infantry.

The young labourer was having none of it. A vicious fight ensued, the outcome of which was that the youth fell to the bottom of the stairs, smashing his skull and dying instantly.

It is at the foot of the stairs in the White Hart that people have experienced an atmosphere of intense fear and dreadful foreboding. Could this be an indelible recording of the emotive panic felt by the youth as he tried to flee his aggressors – a headlong flight that had such dreadful consequences?

Loud voices have also been heard by the White Hart's guests; they state that they seem to initiate from an empty bar, late at night. Yet a third apparition is that of another frightened man. Seen in the 1960's and 1970's, he would seem to confine his meanderings to the bar and one specific bedroom. There has been speculation as to whether or not this could be the unfortunate youth so reluctant to embark on military service. This is thought unlikely by the locals, however, as the scanty reports suggest that this man is in early middle age.

Kings Arms

stone's throw up the street from the White Hart is the ancient Kings Arms. The psychic activity here is enigmatic indeed. It seems to consist of some inexplicable knockings and footsteps. As to the ghostly perpetrator of these sounds, little is actually known, but

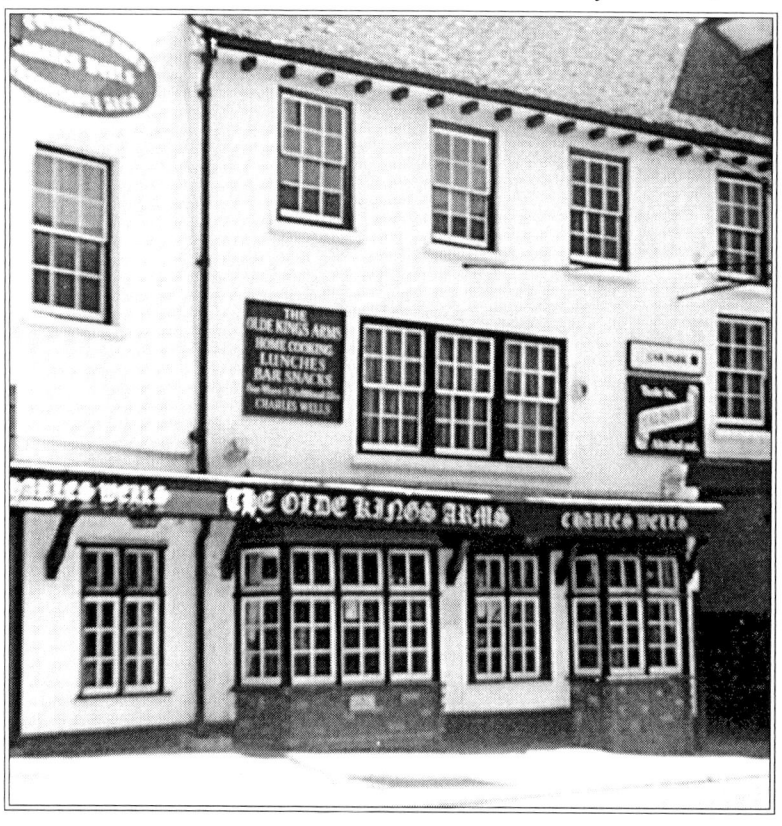

speculation is rife. The old inn has had no shortage of colourful characters in the past but any relationship between them and supernatural footsteps are tenuous.

As long ago as 1628 the Kings Arms was in the news, unfortunately through nothing that enhanced its public image. Abraham Crawley, the landlord, was before the Quarter Sessions for keeping a house of ill repute and for letting his premises be used improperly. There is very little detail and so the outcome of the charge is open to speculation. Crawley does not appear to have lost his licence for in 1630 he reappears, not only as the Kings Arms landlord, but also as Constable of the town.

Crawley's son, also Constable of the town, succeeded his father at the inn and a grandson set up as a solicitor next door, thereby ensuring the family's grasp upon the building and licence, and adding an air of respectability. Crawley is a rather remote possibility as a contender for the phantom footsteps.

In 1756 we find the inn owned by Thomas Kellam, a man with vast influence in the town and as with Crawley, a Chief Constable. Kellam expanded the inn, sharing the yard with the Black Lion, the hostelries together stabling some 60 horses. Kellam's works in Hemel Hempstead are quite well documented and apparently above reproach.

Nothing untoward would seem to have happened during Kellam's long custodianship. Although he is rumoured to meander the corridors of the old building, Kellam would also appear an unlikely contender for spiritual stewardship.

The footsteps, which are becoming less and less frequent, must remain a mystery and the spirit remain anonymous.

NORTHCHURCH

The George and Dragon

est of Hemel Hempstead lies the attractive little town of Berkhampstead and adjoining this, almost a continuation, is the village of Northchurch. The George and Dragon is situated beside the busy A41 where it is at its most lethal.

I was unaware of any phenomena here until it was brought to my notice by Hilary Stainer-Rice in the booklet "Ghosts of the Chilterns". Hilary tells of a George Meager whose spirit seems very loth to leave his favourite chair in the pub. Apparently a new landlord and his wife had noticed the shade of an elderly gentleman walk across the barroom and deposit himself in a seat, soon after to fade from view. Cautiously apprehensive of ridicule, the landlord mentioned the apparition to one or two of his locals including old George's son and daughter-in-law. After a brief description of his spiritual regular, the proprietor was left in no doubt as to his identification. The majority of the small community knew old George and seemed little surprised that he should be enjoying a posthumous pint!

THAME

The Bird Cage Inn

oving further West through the county town of Aylesbury one comes across the delightful market town of Thame. It is one of the few in the country where old and new dwellings reside side by side, at peace in their co-existence.

Probably the most famous building in the town is the Bird Cage Inn. Dating from the 15th century it is most people's archetypal idea of what an old world inn should be. Although the building has been through several architectural changes from its original form, there is more than sufficient of the old building remaining to be of interest. The vast and pleasantly distorted beams, the twisted projecting timbers and the elegant original windows are reminiscent of Walt Disney. A fairy tale creation deposited in an Oxfordshire market town.

As one would expect, the Bird Cage's past is colourful and a little dubious. The vast cellar was once used as a staging prison for French troops during the Napoleonic wars. A whipping post and stocks stood directly outside to encourage the inmates to behave. Up until this time the inn was known as the Blackbird, but after it became the unwelcome quarters of our continental cousins, it became the Bird and Cage. Then through a logical progression to "The Bird Cage".

If the enforced guests in the cellars were unhappy with their lot, they were infinitely better off than the inhabitants of the top floor of the building. There, cramped and crowded in a small room, were a colony of lepers. Leprosy was the scourge of Britain for nearly three centuries. The disease was believed to be far more contagious than it actually was, and those suffering from it were forced to wear a form of cowbell and roam the countryside begging food from those brave enough to approach them.

Some authorities, such as Thame, took a slightly more enlightened view and permitted their local lepers to remain in town, albeit in a much restricted area. The Bird Cage was chosen probably for its height and because its captive audience below could hardly complain. The lepers were locked in a tiny room, there to await approaching death, but sustained by food and water passed in through a trap door on long poles, a job that fell to the brothers of a nearby monastery.

A story based on very little fact but on a plenitude of speculation is that a young leper, sick and tired of being restricted, escaped through the trap door and ran through the town. The appalling disfigurement of the young man shocked the populace into action. Stones were thrown at the leper until he sat in the town centre, head in hands, bleeding profusely, horribly deformed. More and more stones rained down on the poor man's head until finally he fled back to his sanctuary at the top of the Bird Cage Inn, only to die of his wounds there later that evening.

Apparently it is this unfortunate young man that is the unrested spirit at the inn. The paranormal phenomena at the Bird Cage have been occurring for a number of years and are quite well attested.

A couple that took over the inn in the late sixties experienced a cold yet oppressive atmosphere in one of the second floor rooms. Also there was the inevitable knocking. These strange encounters began to endanger the landlady's health and after discussing the matter with regulars, the Society for Psychical Research were contacted. They turned up in force and after some days of diligence the society members detected, or rather experienced, a loud and violent knocking. They managed to ascertain that the disturbance was indeed instigated by the sorrowful leper. A communication system was set up by a simplified Morse code arrangement. A question would be asked and the restless spirit would reply with one knock for the affirmative and two for the negative answer. After hours of this striving, and labour intensive one-sided interview, the investigators were able to interpret that the young man had been stoned to death, that he was an atheist, and that he hated people in general and wished to be left alone.

The phantom's wishes, however, went unheeded for the investigators returned on several occasions. Contact being made, they found the spirit far more annoyed and irritated by the intrusion into his privacy. The questions were answered by such hostile phrases as "leave me alone or I'll kill you".

Once again his appeals were unheeded, in fact his privacy was to be invaded to an even greater extent, this time by a film crew that appeared hoping to do a programme on the paranormal. According to some reports the sound engineer had a variety of troubles with his equipment from the trivial annoyance of a plug being pulled from a socket to a severe or total malfunction of his complete electrical apparatus. All he had been able to record were three words "leave me alone".

How much credence the reader puts on this report is entirely a matter of individual conjecture. Personally I find that all electrical equipment has an independent mind and a strong will of its own, anyway, apart from having an unpredictable if not whimsical nature. The story is good and like all good stories may encourage embellishment as it is retold.

There is, however, a strange rejoinder to the above statement. Sometime after the investigation the landlady was in conversation with a verbose disbeliever in the bar; during the discussion a small mug seemed to take off from its hook and of its own volition fly across the bar towards the sceptic. Unfortunately the landlady chose this moment to alter her position and was struck on the back of the neck. Coincidence? – probably. If not, who was the intended target – the converted or the critic?

The George and Dragon

A fifteen mile drive from Thame down the A4010 will bring the reader to the village of West Wycombe. The village has a timeless quality about it and is a place steeped in history. Probably the most famous of its sons was Sir Francis Dashwood, an eccentric character in the extreme, but also a local benefactor.

Sir Francis was one of an extremely wild bunch, a man of vast influence in the 1760's and 1770's. In 1772 he was made Chancellor of the Exchequer. Although hardly a great man from a moralistic point of view, many of his architectural whims are treasured by the nation.

One of these, a great golden ball, perched high upon a hill above a church, can be seen for miles. Ten men could easily sit inside and the views are spectacular. Besides this gem, he built a mausoleum and beneath it he constructed a labyrinth of caves. The chalk from the caves he utilised in making a well constructed road from the village to the town of High Wycombe three miles away.

For some years local men were employed either in the excavation of the caves or the making of the roadway. This made Dashwood popular with the locals and encouraged them to turn a blind eye to the nefarious goings on once West Wycombe caves had been completed.

The caves were the headquarters of Dashwood's Hell Fire Club, a scandalous brotherhood whose members were generally recruited from London's more opulent and broad-minded society. The avant-garde free thinkers, men not shackled by the inconvenience of morals, priciples or ethics. In fact, the more shocking, the more heinous, the more iniquitous a man's reputation, the higher was his standing in Dashwood's brotherhood.

The stories of the Hell Fire Club have been well documented over the years. The orgies, the debauchery, the sexual perversions enacted with the Medmenham nuns have filled volumes, so it is not my intention to dwell on them here. Let us return to the village. A village so ancient and fascinating that it is now an acquisition of the National Trust.

Near the centre of the village is the tall and gaunt George and Dragon. The Inn was a staging post for the London to Oxford mail and during the Dashwood era was already over 300 years old.

In 1720 a renovation took place and the Inn was given the uniformly accepted façade of a flat brick frontage. At this time the famous massive lead sign was added, a colourful illustration of St George slaying the dragon. The Inn has had a number of spiritual manifestations, the majority of which are obscure and seldom witnessed.

The first one, yet another nun, this time dressed in white, has been occasionally witnessed in the garden. The lady's pedigree is unknown but there is speculation that she is one of Dashwood's friends from Medmenham Abbey. Several were thought to have disappeared during the Hell Fire days but this is once again merely conjecture, an idea supposedly substantiated by the rumour of a tunnel from the George and Dragon to the caves.

The White Nun is one of a quartet of lady spirits at the Inn. Another is a benign and inoffensive lady who has been witnessed by several landladies, sitting in a parlour chair. Yet another (possibly Sukie – who we will talk of later – but possibly not) appears in a white dress. She is a little frightening as the spirit appears at the foot of the bed of some poor guest and "balloons out at you". These are the words of an American visitor named Robbins who was unfortunate enough to encounter the lady whilst staying at the hotel in 1966. He goes on to qualify the statement by likening the apparition to a face reflected in a rounded shiny surface. A similar effect may be encountered by watching one's own face in the reflection of a shiny metal ball swinging first towards one and then away. The American gentleman was quite badly affected by the experience.

Apart from the spirits mentioned above there has also been footsteps on the stairs and some mild poltergeist activity. The activity has been relatively harmless, just the misplacing of certain domestic articles. The gender of these two spirits is unknown, but the moving of articles seems to have the touch of a woman about it.

Then of course there is Sukie (Susan). Sukie is the most famous of all the George and Dragon's manifestations. It has been suggested that she is responsible for all the naughtiness mentioned above and also that she is the composite of all three female apparitions. This is highly unlikely especially in the case of the supposedly celibate sister.

Sukie has a colourful story to tell dated back to the 1770's. She worked as a barmaid at the St George and Dragon at the time when Dashwood had recently completed his caves. She was very attractive and knew it. She used her comeliness to evoke favours from the local lads and farmers. There was always someone about to offer a small present for a sexual encounter. Whereas Sukie was not exactly a prostitute, full or part time, she was an extremely enthusiastic amateur who was not adverse to the odd gratuity.

With the coming of the Hell Fire Club there also came affluence, in the form of London visitors. Gentlemen in fine clothes, ladies in silks and satins bedecked with jewellery were now staying at the Inn, rather than having a fleeting visit whilst the horses were changed on a journey to London or Oxford.

Sukie became ambitious and set her sights on the wealthy young bucks who were visiting rather than the village louts. She began to be a little selective, denying the locals her favours and saving herself for the more promising of the visitors. Sukie was not a fool, she knew her looks were a finite asset and would swiftly forsake her. She wanted a husband, preferably a rich one.

A young man did come into the amorous barmaid's life about this time, an affluent young man, a friend and guest of Sir Francis Dashwood. A man who made a lot of promises in bed. A plausible young gentleman, so much so that Sukie's favours became his and his alone, to the exclusion of all others.

Unfortunately Sukie's monogamous sex life was not at all welcomed by the lads of the village. Since the arrival of her intended, they had been forced into a way of life verging on the celibate. Sukie was getting ideas above her station, Sukie would have to be taught a lesson. An ingenious plan was hatched.

One of the lads had struck up an acquaintance with a scholar in High Wycombe and this gave him the opportunity of getting the young man to write a letter to Sukie purporting to be from her lover. The gist of the letter was that he would be going abroad shortly and wanted to marry her before he went. He would be passing through West Wycombe late that night and would meet her in the Hell Fire Caves with a preacher and witnesses to perform the ceremony.

On receiving the letter Sukie was over the moon. The hours passed by slowly as she sat in her room at the Inn. Evening finally came, a fine drizzle descended. Sukie, adorned in a long white wedding dress, set out from the George and Dragon across the park (incidentally it had been a whim of Dashwood's to design the park in the form of a woman's naked body with the cave entrance in the appropriate place). The fine drizzle had wetted the grass and Sukie's long dress was mud stained and her hair dishevelled as she panted up the steep incline to the entrance of the caves. She finally made it, disordered and untidy but extremely ardent. She clutched a torch from the cave entrance, took some trouble lighting it with a flint. This accomplished, she descended the labyrinth of passages down to the main chamber. Imagine the dark tunnels, the small ineffective light, the young maid periodically calling the name of her lover.

As she reached a smaller chamber about midway to her destination, she passed a large rock. As she did so an unseen hand grabbed her torch and dashed it out. Unearthly screams and hideous shrieks terrified the young maid as the three young lads jumped around her screeching at the top of their voices.

Panic stricken and disorientated, Sukie fled in the darkness. Ribald giggles and hysterical laughter followed her as the youths celebrated the success of their scheme. But tragedy was to follow; Sukie, fleeing in the darkness, tripped over a rock on the uneven floor, dashing her head against the wall of the cave. She lay there motionless as the three lads watched in disbelief. What had started as a silly game had ended in tragedy; Sukie was alive but comatose. One of the lads ran to the village to obtain help. Villagers returned with a makeshift stretcher and bore the luckless maid down to the George and Dragon. Sukie died there in her room in the small hours of the morning. A tragic tale indeed.

Sukie's restless spirit was soon on the scene. The two maids that shared her room at the George and Dragon swore they had had a visitation from their lost colleague only days after the unhappy event. Both steadfastly refused to enter the room again.

Since then Sukie has made regular visits to the Inn. In the elapsed 230 odd years, there have been countless sightings, some as recent as the 1980's. Poor Sukie – will she ever rest, or will she forever search for a husband amongst the customers of the George and Dragon? Most reports of her apparition seem to be in the bedrooms of male guests. Perhaps she feels more at home in these situations?

KNOWL HILL

The Bird in Hand

Leaving West Wycombe and by-passing High Wycombe and Marlow on the A404, then cutting through the village of Burchetts Green, one will arrive at the A4, the Old Bath Road. Head towards Reading and immediately on the right you will come across the Bird in Hand in the village of Knowl Hill.

The haunting of the Bird in Hand is very mysterious indeed. Much of the old building has been altered or demolished. That which remains is mostly hidden by a new motel-type establishment. According to legend a highwayman (name unknown) was celebrating a particularly large haul from a recent raid on a passing coach. Apparently he indulged to too great an extent and then proceeded to fall down the stairs, thereby breaking his neck.

There is little more to tell. Rumour has it that his ghost has been glimpsed from time to time but I can glean no further information, try as I may. It's a pity.

This rather deficient tale ends our spiritual excursion into the Northern and Eastern Chilterns.

· PART THREE ·

The Middle Thames

The Bull

The village of Wargrave has an almost imperceptible bygone charm all of its own. Many of the buildings on and behind its main street are well worth a lingering inspection. That is, of course, if you can find somewhere to park and are not bustled on through the severe bottleneck of houses and swept on your way to Henley by the sheer force of traffic.

There are two old coaching inns on the main street and also two other pubs. All are worth a visit but it is one of the coaching inns, The Bull, which is of particular interest to those seeking the paranormal.

Present owners and customers have seen and heard nothing supernatural but all know the story of the inn.

The Bull has been haunted for some years by the sound of a woman weeping. The eerie mournful sound comes from an upstairs bedroom that is reported to have a strange and uncanny atmosphere. The story concerns a previous landlord from the 1820's who, discovering his wife with a lover, cast her out, forbidding her to come near The Bull or their very young child again. The woman complied with his wishes and several years later died of a broken heart.

The sound of sobbing from the bedroom is the sound of the wretched wife as she is sent packing from the pub. Legend informs that the wailing is far more prevalent on the anniversary of her woeful extradition from the family home. Unfortunately no one can remember just exactly on what day of the year this unhappy event took place.

The George and Dragon

Wargrave is on the river, but one would hardly think so as driving through there is only one fleeting glimpse of it at the northern end of the village. As far as I know this is the only point of access permitted to the public, the rest of the banks being flanked by ornamented but private gardens. The only public approach is at the ferry behind the George and Dragon Inn.

This fine old hostelry has been ruthlessly commercialised and all but destroyed by its being adopted by a steak house company. Alas it has gone the same way as much of our licensed inheritance, its picturesque structure now embellished with massive lime green signs advertising cheap meals. The George and Dragon has no claim to any supernatural occurrences but the river behind it has, albeit a tenuous association.

In the stark chill of 1878 the river was frozen over and locals were skating. A little down river the ice had been smashed to allow the public ferry to operate. The ferry was small and seldom used, a one man operation. A certain Captain Markham came down to skate with his sister and insisted on being taken across. The ferry was half full with frozen water but the ferryman paddled across, along with his two passengers and his small daughter.

The ferry sank, depositing the four into the river; Captain Markham made it to the bank, as did the ferryman. The Captain's sister was pulled out by skaters, in a condition near frozen to death, but the young daughter was lost under the icy water.

There was a tale long ago that the ferryman's small daughter's spirit walked the bank behind the George and Dragon. She only appeared on bitterly cold days and has not been seen for over a century.

The sinking of the boat is an historical fact but the story of the spirit seems more than a little suspect. It could possibly be a case of there being a good opportunity for a ghost, why not invent one?

There is another very unlikely spiritual character just on the river, or rather in the river. His name is Bingy or Bengy. He seems to be a mysterious sprite after the fashion of Robert Goodfellow. Bingy entices people into the river to drown. How he quite manages this is not revealed, but he seems to take the blame for many small disasters.

The Little Angel

O n the road towards Henley at a junction where the Wargrave Road meets the Maidenhead Road, stands the Little Angel.

Mary Blandy, a 30 year old spinster of Henley, was accused and convicted of patricide in 1752. It is a long and involved story that I have tried to do justice to in "I'll be Hanged". There has always been some doubt as to Mary's guilt. It was alleged that she, with her fiancé Captain Willie Cranstoun,

administered arsenic to her father. Willie fled abroad helped by wealthy and influential associates. Mary had to stay and face the music.

Whilst an autopsy was being performed on her deceased parent, Mary was locked in her room above in the family home in Hart Street, Henley. The door had been locked for several days, her meals brought in by one faithful servant. Her shoe buckles and laces were removed in case she did herself any bodily harm.

Towards the evening of her third day of house arrest, Mary Blandy tried her bedroom door and found to her surprise that it had inadvertently been left unlocked. More out of lust for fresh air than a bid for freedom, Mary walked out into the busy Hart Street and headed towards Henley Bridge. She had often enjoyed a walk at Park Place, Remenham on the Berkshire side of the river, and this no doubt was her intent.

Unfortunately for Mary, her private life had been public property since the death of her father. Biased gossip and accusations had spread like wildfire round the small town of Henley. Already penny newspapers were circulating in London and Oxford describing the murder in the first person as if written by Mary. As far as the public were concerned, she was tried and convicted before actually being formally charged.

As Mary walked through the busy market, she was immediately recognised and the hue and cry went up , "There's Mary Blandy the murderess!", a statement followed by a missile from a small boy. "There's Mary Blandy the poisoner!" women joined in the chant as they bartered for goods.

Mary quickened her pace, her buckle-less shoes slipping as she attempted an embarrassed escape from the scorn of the townsfolk. "After the murderess, she's escaping!" Mary headed for the bridge as fast as her distorted footwear and long dress would permit her. The crowd followed hurling abuse, stones and vegetables.

Alarmed, she fled across the bridge just yards ahead of the screaming mob. In panic she reached the Berkshire bank and hammered on the door of the Angel. The landlady, a long time friend of Mary's, let her in and bolted the door behind her. Once inside, the young spinster collapsed onto the nearby couch in a state of hysteria whilst the disappointed mob, denied its prey, settled for shouting profanities from the street outside.

After some time the town constable Richard Fisher arrived and dispersed the mob, also taking Mary into official custody. He placed her in a stage coach for Oxford where she was to spend some months awaiting trial. Mary Blandy was convicted, sentenced and hanged at Oxford in 1752.

There are three sites near Henley that are rumoured to be frequented by the spirit of Mary. One is the old family home in Hart Street. The second is the Kenton Theatre where any amount of poltergeist activity was reputed to go on when an attempt to stage the play "The Hanging Wood" takes place. The production is the story of Mary Blandy's life.

The third venue, over the bridge in Remenham, is the Little Angel. There have been reports, admittedly some years ago, of hammering on the front door. The rappings are assumed to be the unfortunate Mary as she tries to obtain sanctuary from the howling mob.

A second apparition, once again not witnessed for some time, again thought to be Mary, is the manifestation of a hysterical lady sitting on a couch. The Little Angel is a popular pub today, extremely busy with businessmen consuming appetising lunches – hardly an atmosphere conducive with the spirit of Henley's sad and sombre spinster.

The Bull

O ver the bridge from Remenham is the town of Henley. Famous for its regatta and its opulent riverside properties the town has an abundance of ancient inns. One such inn, The Bull in Bell Street, is arguably the oldest and the most picturesque. The frontage is cabled and has an overhanging first floor. The historic exterior seems completely at odds with its glass and plastic younger neighbours.

There is little known of the spiritual figure that is said to frequent one of the bedrooms. It is yet another cowled visitor, obviously a monk, but why he should frequent The Bull is unknown. The manifestation is usually preceded by a smell of burning candles. There is nothing more to be said, the apparition is harmless and becoming more and more infrequent.

PISHILL

The Crown

ollowing on from Henley's Bell Street is the main road to Oxford. A couple of miles outside the town a secondary road leads off to the right in the direction of Watlington. After passing the vast grounds of Stonor Park one comes across the delightful village of Pishill, a hamlet that rivals Piddle-hampton in Dorset as the butt of lewd witticisms. The name, however, is thought to have been initiated from a family of French gentry who inhabited the area, whose surname was Pis.

Coming upon The Crown when turning a bend in the narrow road gives one a feeling of veneration of almost awe inspired solemnity.

This is chocolate box, Tudor beauty at its best. There can be few more attractive inns in the country. The exterior is covered by a profusion of wisteria. There is a charming garden and a converted barn with an enormous thatched roof strewn with roses and hollyhocks.

The Crown is reputed to possess the largest priest hole in the country, but even so that isn't to say that it is vast. Priest holes were notoriously tiny places, usually concealed near chimney breasts. Not for the faint hearted or claustrophobic were these hideaways where Jesuits often sat for days, their food and water being passed in surreptitiously by their frightened but dedicated supporters.

There is a romantic tale attached to the priest hole at The Crown. A fugitive priest, thought to be named Dominique, left his place of concealment for clandestine meetings with an attractive lady guest at the inn. He would watch from his hiding place until the husband had left and would then shin down a rope for his and the lady's mutual satisfaction. Inevitably he was caught in a compromising position and immediately run through by the aggrieved husband's sword.

Loud footsteps and insistent thumping at the inn have been attributed to the luckless Dominique. But this could once again be a case of the conditions and venue being conducive with a fictional legend.

WALLINGFORD

The George Hotel

I t is a brief drive from Pishill to the small and thriving town of Wallingford. The George is a prominent building in the High Street. It is known that a man was murdered at the old inn as far back as 1626 but it is not his shade that is said to haunt the place.

There is a strange feature in one of the bedrooms. Known as the teardrop room it has a strange decor. One wall has an unusual painted plasterwork design which has been likened to large teardrops. The embossed globules resembling closely the shape of tears has given rise to intense speculation.

It is rumoured (date unspecified) that a previous landlord's daughter was infatuated by a young man of the town. The couple were due to be married and prospects looked good. Unfortunately the young man was brutally murdered, some accounts state that he was bludgeoned to death after disturbing burglars on his property.

On hearing the sad news the landlord's daughter grieved herself into insanity. She had to be confined to her room, where, her mind in such disarray, she spent the rest of her days painting this weird mural, her design constructed from tears and soot, her paintbrush, her finger.

Several guests have witnessed the weeping woman and have given quite graphic accounts. She appears almost life-like with such apparent substance that several have taken her to be a member of staff. The apparition soon fades, however, and disappears into the masonry of the teardrop wall, leaving the startled observer with an overpowering feeling of depression and remorse.

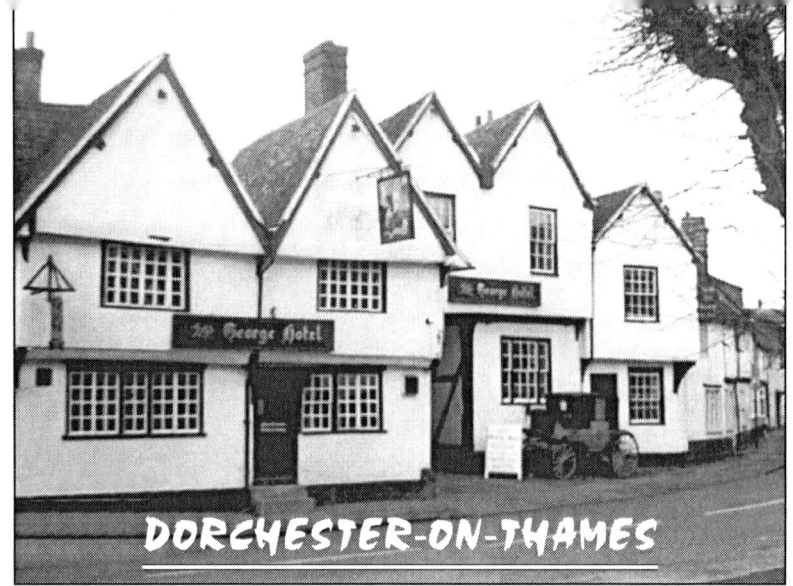

The George

A trip of 4 or 5 miles up the A423 will bring the reader to the ancient village of Dorchester. It is difficult to visualise that this collection of pristine old buildings was once a mighty city.

The heyday of Dorchester-on-Thames was over a thousand years ago when it was the capital city of Mercia. It then boasted a cathedral, a monastery, an abbey and a plethora of churches.

Now only the abbey remains and opposite stands the ancient George Hotel, majestic and benign. The George stands on the site of the original abbey hospice and is without doubt one of the oldest inns in the country.

For a hostelry with such a long and colourful past, it has surprisingly, only one spiritual visitor. One would have expected more from a watering hole that has been around in some form or other since 1140. The spirit is that of a lady in white who haunts the strangely named "Vicar's Room". She is a very mournful and dour looking individual who appears at the corner of a four poster bed and then simply turns her back and vanishes. Once again there is nothing known of the identity of the said lady, what causes her grief, or who she may have been in a former existence.

CLIFTON HAMDEN

The Plough

arrying on towards Oxford on the A423, turn left on the A415 and you will come across the village of Clifton Hamden. The Plough, an ancient and thatched hostelry, stands on the right near a T-junction.

In the mid-sixties there were reports of mild but prolific poltergeist activity in this pub. Glasses turned upside down of their own volition, emptying their contents over the floor. There were also reports by customers of apparitions that silently travelled the passages. A strange penetrating blue light like the beam of a laser was also described by various customers.

But possibly the most lovable of the Plough's spirits is the "Phantom Nudger". Reputedly the earthbound spirit of an ex-landlord's dog, Nudger comes along the bar pushing his nose into people's backsides to attract their attention – a trick he used to be particularly fond of, apparently. He liked a pat on the head as a response. Just turn and pat where you think the nudge came from – you might look an idiot, but you'll be keeping a deceased doggie in high spirits!

The Blueberry Inn

A complicated system of minor roads will take the motorist through Long Wittenham to pick up the B4016 at Appleford. More twists and turns on this narrow road will finally bring one to Blewbury, a pleasant village straddling the main Reading to Wantage Road. Blewbury is best seen at a leisurely pace, preferably on foot. Its ancient thatched walls and grassed orchards have a friendly and comforting quality. It has the tranquil serenity often denied to more spectacular beauty.

At the Western end of the village lies the Blueberry Inn. Since the 1790's the establishment has rejoiced in the varying names of the King William, the Blewbury Inn and The New Inn.

In the coaching era the old place had a more than sinister reputation, as a number of its overnight guests disappeared, the eccentric landlord planting fruit trees over the unfortunate travellers' graves after he had robbed and murdered them. Possibly this action put more body in the soil, thereby enhancing the produce.

Contrary to what one might expect it is not the spirit of the murdering landlord that makes visitations to the inn. Nor is it one of his hapless victims. It is in fact a very benign and amiable phantom. The spirit of the Blueberry Inn belongs to an ex-landlord who died some 40 years ago. His footsteps may be heard late at night moving from his bedroom and down into the bar. It would seem that he is securing the premises, as conscientious in death as he was in life.

❖ ❖ ❖

The Bull

aking the A417 towards Reading will bring you to the captivating riverside village of Streatley. The Bull stands beside the main road and has done for some 500 years. In 1833 the murderer George King was being transported from Wantage to Reading to stand trial. King, a farm labourer, had slaughtered the landlady at the White Hart at Wantage by completely decapitating her with a beanhook. It was the most horrendous of crimes and all for the few shillings in the landlady's purse. A complete report of this heinous murder can be read in detail in "Well I'll be Hanged".

Although the evidence was overwhelmingly staked against him, King stubbornly refused to confess. However, when the constable's coach stopped for refreshment at The Bull, King suddenly noticed a picture of a middle aged woman hanging in the bar.

The picture had a vague likeness of Ann Pullin, King's unfortunate victim. He took this as an omen and began to shake and become increasingly alarmed. "It's her, Mrs Pullin, she's following me. I'll kill her again," he screamed. The constables held the young farm hand as he hysterically stuttered out a confession before a surprised landlord and customers.

The supernatural reports at the Bull have absolutely nothing to do with the distraught murderer. They are far, far older and more indistinct. The story however is a romantic one.

The legend relates that in the early 1500's a monk was having secret assignations with a novice from a nearby nunnery. The Bull was the selected venue for these covert meetings, meetings that were as passionate as they were short-lived. Discovered, they were slain on the spot and buried beneath two massive yew trees in the garden.

For years it was rumoured that on balmy summer nights the lover spirits forsook their lonely graves and walked hand in hand through the garden.

The infatuated couple have not been seen for some years. If indeed they ever were. Still, it's a nice story.

With this fanciful story we conclude this tour of the Middle Thames area.

· PART FOUR ·

Reading and Around

HURST

The Castle Inn

little difficult to find in an extremely widespread village is the Castle at Hurst. The Castle Inn, once called the Church House, is old indeed, and looks it. It has an oven in the lounge that once baked bread for the whole village. It supposedly has an underground tunnel to the church opposite, and it has a ghost, or possibly two. Noises have been heard by various tenants over the years, usually at night and always indistinguishable. As far as I can ascertain, nothing has even been seen.

The Inn has a pretty colourful history, if more than a little enigmatic. A young woman is thought to have died in the quaintly named Coffin Room, a place where the dead were laid out awaiting burial in the neighbouring churchyard. Also autopsies were often carried out at local inns.

A young boy is reported as having committed suicide in this room but the facts are obscure to say the least. Whether both or either of these unfortunate souls are responsible for the strange rumbling is open to conjecture.

George Hotel

umerous signposts from Hurst will take one into the centre of Reading. In a town virtually bereft of any interesting old architecture. The George Hotel is one of the few gems of interest in the centre of Reading. Unfortunately now a steak house, it was once an old coaching inn. The gabled overhead entrance, the cobbled courtyard with its 18th century coach, bear witness to the George's colourful and functional past.

I only heard of any supernatural phenomena after reading of it in Joan Foreman's "The Haunted South". The authoress's enquiries could glean only the most sketchy information and my casual references to various members of staff fared no better.

The haunting, or more correctly the atmosphere, is experienced in one of the older upstairs bedrooms. It is apparently a feeling of great depression. There would seem to be no perceptible cause. No dastardly deeds have been known to have happened at the inn. I am sorry but there is little to add.

READING

The Roebuck

From the centre of Reading follow the Oxford Road. This is an extremely long and tedious street, lined with small businesses and shops of every description. It is also a very popular practice ground for every local authority. Gas, electricity, water and various other boards regularly take it in turns to excavate the road, thereby adding to the already horrendous traffic turmoil.

After the final Reading roundabouts, head towards Pangbourne on the A329. The Roebuck appears on the right hand side. Not even the most generous of writers could ever

describe it as an attractive pub. It is bleak, bare and unembellished.

Much of the history of the Roebuck is unknown. It is rumoured that it was once the home of a retired admiral but none of the previous researchers have ever been able to ascertain his name. One would think that there would be a record somewhere. Be that as it may, it is this unnamed naval officer who is deemed responsible for the playful poltergeist activity at the inn. Legend dictates that the admiral died under very suspicious circumstances and possibly this is the reason for his unsettled spirit. A former landlord claimed that locked doors and windows were opened and furniture moved mysteriously. Heavy footsteps were heard late at night, both along the corridors and on the gravel outside. Dogs have refused to enter certain rooms. Some researchers look upon this as an acid test as to whether or not there is any paranormal activity. I personally believe this is because of a dog's naturally suspicious nature.

But to return to the phantom admiral. It would appear that he has never been seen and that his frolicsome activities have lessened considerably over the years. In fact nothing supernatural has been experienced for some time.

YATTENDON

The Royal Oak

left turn in Pangbourne and a right turn in Tidmarsh signposted Yattendon will take the traveller way up into the hills and eventually to the Royal Oak.

The Royal Oak has won several awards for its hospitality and its spruce and shipshape exterior. It is always given the highest acclaim in all the famous guides to inns and hotels.

There is a very sad story here of a lady falling to her death some time in the 1950's. She fell into a disused and unknown well shaft. There are many such wells in the area, most of them now filled in. I am told that the council did a survey to try and trace them. They found a goodly number, but one they didn't find is the legendary well located somewhere in a farmer's field. It supposedly holds the villagers' treasure, hurriedly deposited when they fled Cromwell's advancing troops during the civil war. There have been treasure hunters over the years but they have been deterred by a ghostly figure that is thought to mislead them if they are getting too close to the villagers' hoard.

The Royal Oak's supernatural manifestations seem to have died a natural death nearly forty years ago. They were never attributed to the unfortunate lady as they ceased before her demise. They were just a few rumblings and bumps that seemed to lessen and finally faded away. Possibly earth moving in the 140 undiscovered well shafts may have been in no small way responsible.

The Old Boot Inn

 everal slightly confusing signposts will lead the traveller under the M4 to the village of Standford Dingley. Of the village's two inns, one would expect the aged Bull to be the more conducive to supernatural experiences. But this is not so. It is the far newer Boot that has experienced some sort of mild psychic phenomena. Once again doors and drawers open and close mysteriously. The ghostly perpetrator of the action is rumoured to be an unfortunate suicide, a local man who hanged himself in the pub's orchard.

❖ ❖ ❖

ALDERMASTON

The Butt Inn

ack roads through Beenam and across the A4 bring us to Aldermaston, a village made famous in the sixties by "Ban the Bomb" demonstrations. Situated by itself as you approach the village, there is another ancient pub, the Butt Inn.

Whilst compiling this book, I have made it a practice never to ask the landlord directly about any paranormal incidents attached to the house. The reasons are various: they are generally too busy and have no reticence about telling you so; they often deny all knowledge for fear of being ridiculed or because they are sick and tired of answering previous enquiries; or they tell you what they think you want to hear by embellishing and exaggerating the facts.

With the Butt Inn I made an exception to the rule. After a polite discussion about the age of the property (some 500 years), I casually asked if it were haunted.

"Oh yes," he replied, but did not elaborate.

"By whom?" I asked without enthusiasm, having found in the past that a very casual enquiry brings the best results. "A lady ghost, a gentleman, or what?" I continued.

"Whatever *it* is" (he emphasised the word "it"), "It turns on beer taps and slams doors," he replied.

The landlord would be drawn no further and I went away wondering if he had been joking or not. Most perplexing. A thought-provoking little episode for my final call in this brief trip around the Reading and district pubs.

· PART FIVE ·

Wokingham, Bracknell and Around

Ye Olde Rose Inne

O pposite the old town hall in the centre of Wokingham is the imposing but fake facade of Ye Olde Rose Inn. The Rose is one of the oldest of the town's fast diminishing prolific population of pubs. As recently as the early 60's there were 34 in this small town, including 14 within 200 yards of the town hall. Alas, many have given way to supermarkets, car parks, shoe shops and various other non-essential establishments.

To be fair to the Rose it was a genuine Elizabethan inn. The counterfeit frontage tries to emulate as closely as possible the original design. It was necessitated by one of three mysterious fires that broke out in the early seventies almost totally destroying the building.

Much of the interior of the Rose has been restored by the steak house group that now own the building. The owners have tried their best to recreate an atmosphere but are inevitably doomed to failure.

An atmosphere that was enjoyed in the 16th century by Alexander Pope, one of the most sensual, far thinking and philosophical of our poets. He made one of his regular calls to the inn one day accompanied by his equally famous friends Arbuthnot, Gay and Swift. Here they concocted between them "The Ballad of Molly Mogg" in honour of a barmaid at the Rose, famous throughout the neighbourhood for her beauty. One wonders how the poets' train of thought would have been if it had been constantly interrupted by a blaring intercom blandly announcing, "Mr Smith, your table for two is now ready."

The Rose has a ghost. It is a serving maid but not Molly Mogg, I hasten to add. This lady was some two hundred years later in the early 1800's. In life she was a young and innocent girl, made pregnant by the 19th century equivalent of a travelling salesman. He didn't return. She could not live with the disgrace and hanged herself. Since then her spirit has been reported in the dining rooms. Her visits have been intermittent and do not seem to commemorate the anniversary of the untimely death.

The more romantic and fanciful reporters of this sad shade blame the poor maid for the three mysterious fires. Balderdash! If logic exists in the spirit world, why should this poor unhappy spectre be quite content to harmlessly float through kitchen and restaurants for some 150 years and then become a raging pyromaniac for a brief 15 years in the 60's and early 70's? – most unlikely.

Having said this, there is a very strange occurrence reported in the late 80's. A friend of mine swears that one evening he was dining in the upstairs restaurant when a table lamp moved its way between the plates and across the table, only stopping when it had come to the end of its length of electric cable. He vows that it moved of its own volition, was watched by at least four diners, and was not in the vicinity of any human hand. Strange indeed – another enigma.

BRACKNELL

South Hill Park Bar

L eaving behind the ancient market town of Wokingham and travelling four miles east, one will come across the far more modern metropolis of Bracknell. Although small pockets of earlier architecture can be observed, Bracknell remains a brainchild of the 1950's when a dozen or so of its kin were constructed for the overspill of the capital and labelled "New Towns".

Following the Crowthorne signposts from the centre one catches a glimpse of a large 18th century house on the left hand side. This is South Hill Park, now an arts centre but also possessing a cinema, theatre and several bars.

Readers have no doubt noticed that I have been extremely liberal in my interpretation of reputedly haunted "pubs". It could not have escaped one's notice that under this general heading I have also encompassed Inns, Hotels, Winebars and Restaurants – in fact any outlet that serves alcoholic beverages to the general public. This is the one qualification and it enables me to include the bar at South Hill Park.

When I was a child, I spent many an hour climbing the trees in South Hill Park; they were many and varied, some all but unique to this country. The main factors they seemed to have in common were that they were massive and twisted into every conceivable shape. The old place (for much of its history uninhabited) had an air of mystery about it and I was not surprised to hear the many and varied stories of haunting associated with it.

In the early 1920's a Major Rickman, OBE, inherited the property from his old aunt Mrs Haversham. Unfortunately for the Major, he also inherited a vast debt. He tried for some time to elevate himself from the mounting financial encumbrance, but finding the burden too awesome, he capitulated by fatally shooting himself in the gun room. The story expounded soon after his death was that the spectre of the Major walked the veranda at the back of the house.

In my childhood days many a mischievous child would rout his companions from scrumping with knee-skinning speed by hollering at the top of his voice, "Here comes the phantom Major!" Major Rickman's veranda is now a very popular bar area and in the summer it is swarming with people who appreciate the lush green gardens that surround it. Ghosts, I am led to believe, are notoriously shy of crowds, so it is little wonder that the Major has not made his presence felt for a number of years.

There are various other psychic phenomena in other parts of the old building, all of a much later date. Security guards in the 80's have experienced strange goings-on in one particular dressing room. The door closes on its own when there is not the slightest wind, lights have been seen in the room from outside the building when none exist. There is also the uncanny feeling of being watched.

Other people have heard dreary whistling noises and the whining sounds of cats at war, but have found it impossible to trace the source of such laments. There is also a sudden, inexplicable fall of temperature in one of the corridors.

All very indistinct and suspect, one might think, a catalogue of half truths that may or may not have perfectly plausible and mundane explanations, but Jeffrey Nicholls in his booklet "Our Mysterious Shire" related a more individual and specific occurrence. It concerns a lady who was working in the studio theatre one February evening in the early 1980's; she was arranging some props which consisted of a table and a heavy velvet tablecloth. The lady carried the table to the centre of the theatre, leaving the cloth neatly folded on the floor. When she turned to fetch the table cloth, she found that it had followed her and was now only several yards behind her, suspended in mid-air. After a few minutes it fell, and, I quote, "not fast, like an unaided object – it seemed to drift down as if held by invisible hands".

This strange occurrence has been associated with a spectral child that is rumoured to exist in the theatre area. The play that was about to be put on had an entire cast of children. The witness puts forward the rather fanciful idea that this ghostly elfin had a wish to be involved in some small way, thereby assisting with the props.

Mr Nicholls, who takes his ghost hunting seriously, then relates how he spent the night at South Hill Park and recorded several unexplained noises and experienced a sudden drop in temperature. He remains, as I do, very open minded.

BRACKNELL

The Horse and Groom

ontinuing in towards the centre of Bracknell along the Bagshot Road, the traveller will find "The Horse and Groom" near to a large roundabout. Unfortunately this old inn is yet another victim of a national steak house corporation.

When I was researching my second book I accidentally came across a Bracknell murder whilst scrutinising copies of the Reading Mercury dating from the early 1800's. I have lived in the Bracknell area all of my life and was surprised that none of the many and varied guides and histories of the town had ever made reference to it. The Reading Mercury of October 15th 1810 informs us that an inquisition was held at the Horse and Groom, Bracknell, concerning the body of one William Ware. William, a youth of 17, was returning to Frimley with his father and two friends from Bracknell Fair. Near Bagshot Heath

the party was set upon by three men, thought to be Irishmen, who beat them with cudgels for some considerable time. The unhappy party returned to the inn, where William died from his wounds a day later. The jury brought in a verdict of wilful murder by persons unknown.

No further information came to light, this brief account was the sole media coverage of William Ware's young life and untimely death, another footstep in the sands of time.

Whether the virtually unknown and unfortunate adolescent from Frimley is responsible for the psychic phenomena at the Horse and Groom is debatable. According to an ex-landlord who was resident at the inn for a number of years, he certainly is not.

Mr Ray George, the landlord involved, found in the early days at the Horse and Groom that a spirits cupboard, to which he had the only keys, was often found to be unlocked. A phantom tippler was at work. I naturally suggested that one of the staff he had inherited from the previous tenant may have found it prudent to have had his own keys made, thereby giving him access to the occasional clandestine tot of whiskey.

I was informed that this was most unlikely as he had brought most of his own staff with him and that the door was still discovered to be open after he had changed the lock. Strange indeed.

There is also a strong rumour of a second spirit at the Horse and Groom, a benign old lady who inhabits an upstairs room and is no bother to anybody at all. Most of the staff in the late 1960's were on nodding acquaintance with her, as with a close neighbour who wanted people to respect her privacy.

However, new babysitters took a little time to adjust to the old lady's footsteps overhead as she busied herself with domestic chores.

Little has been heard of this resident spirit for some time. She had probably been shuffled from her earthbound home by the speed and noise of a 1990's steak house and has finally opted for some type of spirits' retirement home.

BRACKNELL

The Old Manor and the Hind's Head

he Hind's Head once stood at the top of Bracknell High Street some forty or fifty yards from the Old Manor. The Inn was ancient indeed and was reputed to be a watering hole of Dick Turpin's. But then, where didn't? If all the claimants of this dubious honour were to be believed, the highwayman must have lived in a permanent stupor, staggering his way from one hostelry to another.

The Hind's Head was demolished in the early sixties. I had the misfortune of being one of the crew that pulled the old place down. I even hid the sign under some bricks to retrieve later. Unfortunately somebody else had the same idea, for when I returned it was gone (or could this have been the power of some supernatural force?). The following is a pasage from my second book:

"The story proliferated about the old inn is that in the 1770's it was owned by a couple named Milliard. This pair subsidised their living by murdering any visitor that stayed overnight, availing themselves of their victims' personal belongings and then depositing their bodies in a nearby well. The story related that the couple were finally caught and hanged. There would seem little evidence to substantiate the story, or the myth, that there is a tunnel between the Hind's Head and the Old Manor. There was no doubt a well at the Hind's Head and credence was given to an unlikely story that the victims' bones were discovered in it. The bones were probably the remains of animals that had died. One hopes they were deposited after the well ceased to be the inn's main water supply. The subterranean passage may also have been in existence as both buildings were extremely old and priest holes have certainly been found in the Old Manor. In fact one of them is exhibited in one of the bars. A brown cassocked priest gazes down with envy at the imbibers. More likely though, is that the Hind's Head, along with many inns of its day, had a long and narrow wine cellar. Later on most of these were deemed unnecessary and were bricked up. No doubt this has given rise to many a legendary tale; there is nothing so romantic and enticing as a secret passage.

If the Milliards did exist, and were hanged for their nefarious actions, it certainly was not in the 1770's. By that time all Berkshire murderers were despatched from Reading, and there is certainly no record of anybody named Milliard paying the ultimate price between 1770 and 1800. If the couple did exist, they must have purveyed their iniquitous business long before the 1770's."

Unlike the Hind's Head, the Old Manor is still standing and apparently thriving, albeit as yet another steak house. There have been reports here of cowled figures and indistinct chanting for many years, but nothing that the factual student could get to grips with. There is very little primary evidence. Much is clouded by hearsay.

Leaving aside the cowled figure that might or might not have been a Jesuit priest from one of the several priest holes, there was a second and altogether different apparition witnessed

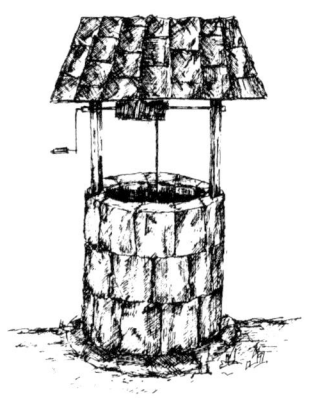

here in the early 1970's. It was the spiritual manifestation of a regular who used the inn as a local. I remember the man well, large, portly, red faced with a handlebar moustache, he was a larger than life character, never seen without his much adorned checkered hat. His apparition shortly after his death startled several of the bar staff at the Old Manor. One attempted to serve him in his regular seat, but as she enquired of his order, he promptly disappeared before her eyes.

This gentleman seems to have made fewer and fewer appearances over the years, but any strange or seemingly inexplicable occurrence is put down to this chap whom the bar staff have nicknamed Fred. This second christening confuses those of us that knew the chap in human form. We all called him Bert.

❖ ❖ ❖

The Royal Ascot Hotel and Berystede Hotel

L eaving Bracknell on the Ascot Road (A329), after several miles, the driver will come across a large roundabout just before entering the village of Ascot. Here once stood the Royal Ascot Hotel. It was demolished in the 1960's to make way for road widening and a vast and very expensive housing estate. The old place was haunted by the sounds of a galloping horse. It seemed to clatter into a cobbled yard, pull to a halt and then whinny and blow hard. Nobody ever knew if there

was a story attached to it, and if my memory serves me well, there was never a cobbled yard at the Royal Ascot.

However, the place was even older than I am, and trying to trace a horse at Ascot would be verging on lunacy, so this equine spirit must remain a mystery.

There are, however, still locals at Ascot who test my gullibility to the extreme by stating that the footsteps may still be heard if one listens intently at the grass verge where once the hotel's stables were. They promise they will keep "an ear to the ground" for further information.

Driving on into the centre of Ascot and turning right at the Horse and Groom for South Ascot and the Railway Station, passing the station and the village, the road extends to Sunninghill. The Berystede Hotel is a large, attractive building on the right on the outskirts of the village. On this site once stood the handsome country home of the Standish family, one of the most opulent in an area famous for opulent houses.

On the morning of 27th October 1886 this palatial mansion caught fire. In a short time it was completely gutted. The charred remains of Eliza Kleineger, Mrs Standish's French maid was found at the bottom of the servants' staircase.

Over the years this elderly woman had collected jewels and trinkets, presents from previous employers she had amassed over decades. It is thought that Eliza may well have originally escaped the flames but had returned for her priceless baubles. Then being trapped by blazing timbers, had succumbed to the smoke, finally to expire in the inferno.

Rebuilt as an hotel, staff and guests soon found that Eliza had retained her position. Her ghost was often witnessed under the central gable where the old servants' staircase used to be. She appears as a withered and worrying spirit, dithering and apprehensive. Perhaps the little French maid is still searching for her treasured hoard?

Rackstraws

L eaving Sunninghill and joining the A30, head in a Westerly direction, travelling through Camberley and turning right into Sandhurst, Rackstraws (now called Treetops) can be found on the right hand side near the centre of the village.

Rackstraws, once an old farmhouse, is now a restaurant, bar and nightclub complex, but much of the original building still remains. In the front bar is a large old-fashioned fireplace with an oven behind. Soon after the opening in the eighties, the oven was photographed for added publicity, probably for a brochure or menu cover.

When the film was developed, there appeared in the picture, quite clearly defined, in the recess of the oven, a skull!

I am fully aware of the sceptical reaction aroused in most people by photographs of the unknown; there has been so much jiggery-pokery and chicanery over the years, and photographs are so easy to fake, that there is never any way of telling whether a particular picture is authentic or not. One can only evaluate the evidence and opt for the most plausible of the variables. That this photograph (once on display in the bar) is genuine, I am prepared to believe. For one reason, several people who have no reason to lie have stated to me the facts and for another, if it had been staged, a far better job could have been made of it.

I should like to be able to relate a picturesque and colourful tale of travellers being waylaid and murdered at the old farmhouse and of bodies hidden in priest holes or even recesses, but I cannot. As far as I know the farm was a perfectly respectable and hard working abode – or was it?

SANDHURST

Duke's Head

andhurst is one of the country's longest villages, almost three miles from end to end. If the main road is followed through laborious twists and turns towards Wokingham, the traveller finally arrives at the Duke's Head on the right hand side. The Duke's Head is one of two pubs that face one another, the other being the Rose and Crown.

I do not believe there have been any supernatural occurrences for some time, but there certainly were many years ago.

My grandparents lived a short way up New Road in a house named St Faith's, opposite the long terrace that was all part of the Duke's Head. Grandfather was the first car owner and motor mechanic in the village and opened a small garage and workshop next door to the Rose and Crown. Later petrol pumps were added, but Grandad, who to say the least imbibed a little, often let the tanks run dry, his downfall being the close proximity of two licensed premises to his business.

At this time, just after the first world war, the Duke's Head was run by a family named Blake. When Mr Blake died, leaving a wife and three daughters, the family found it impossible to carry on with the business and left the premises. One of Mrs Blake's daughters, admittedly a girl that was retarded, would lie in her room at the inn staring directly at the ceiling corner as if mesmerised. She reported that shapes of people manifested themselves there.

Little enough on its own, one must admit, but when Mrs Blake left the pub she moved in with my grandmother as a lodger. With grandfather's cavalier attitude towards business and the added drain on resources of his insatiable thirst, the money came in very handy. Whilst lodging at St Faith's, Mrs

Blake informed grandma that several guests had seen strange shapes there and some found the atmosphere intolerable.

Another lodger my grandmother inherited from the Duke's Head was a Mrs King or Kingdom. She had also experienced some strange phenomena at the room in the old inn. There is a story attached to Mrs King that does not involve the supernatural but is still worth briefly repeating. The old lady had been a lady's maid most of her life and on her own admission had met a lot of shady characters over the years. She was once on very friendly terms with "The Devil Man Charlie Peace".

There has been more poetic licence used by local authors about Charlie Peace than any other notorious character in history. Yateley, two miles south of Sandhurst, has virtually adopted him. Landlords will show you ale mugs that he used and several houses in the neighbourhood claim to have been his abode.

In fact Charlie was in Yateley for only a couple of months whilst he was on the run, and he was far from the dashing highwayman that some local authors project as his image. He was born in Yorkshire in 1833, a grotesque little man (5' 2") with a deformed arm and a mouth that continually dribbled through a tongue that seemed far too big for it. Charlie committed two horrendous and cowardly murders, one of a police officer, and literally dozens of burglaries.

Charlie was hanged at Leeds in 1879, aged 46. Mrs King was presented with some gold and ivory cameos by Charlie when she was a young maid at a large house in Blackheath. There must have been a good deal of affection there for Peace was not renowned for his generosity. In fact there is quite strong testimony that Charlie only came to this area because he felt sure he would be safe in a large house in Yateley owned by a well known local family. Mrs King was once again housemaid there.

In 1923 when Mrs King left her lodgings she presented my grandmother with these cameos. Once, when times were particularly hard, she took them to Reading with the idea of pawning them, but a terrified pawnbroker ushered her quickly from his shop. "I couldn't possibly touch those," he said.

Whether his attitude of quiet panic was due to the enormous value of the cameos, or whether they were famous and on some wanted list, we shall never know, but my grandmother never tried to pawn them again. They remained with her until her death in 1932, but they disappeared after her demise.

When chattering to an ex-landlord's son the other day, he told me another strange story that I admit I had not heard of before. Prior to the alterations, the large front bar was once two smaller ones, the old fashioned "public and lounge" which were invariably the norm of every country pub. The bar was curved so that it could serve either room, with a small "bottle and jug" in the centre that met one on entry. It was an easy matter to look from the lounge into the mirror behind the bar and observe the greater part of the public bar.

In the late 1970's the landlord had friends staying with him and they were prone to have a mid-morning drink in the lounge bar. At that time of day things were generally very quiet and often the public bar was deserted. On noticing a small trilbied man in the public bar by seeing his reflection in the mirror, the landlord's friends walked round to have a chat and possibly make themselves known to the locals and learn a little about the neighbourhood.

On reaching the public bar they found it was, in fact, deserted and yet there would seem to have been no exit other than the communal one in the hallway between the two bars.

Strange indeed, but the couple thought no more of it until a similar thing happened the following day. They spied the little man, blackcoated and trilbied, enjoying a pint at the bar. They quickly walked round, but once again he had gone.

On relating this story to the landlord and other locals and then describing the shy imbiber in as much detail as they could remember, the couple were informed that, without a doubt, this was the shade of a regular who had died some years previously. The description was perfect.

FINCHAMPSTEAD

The Queen's Oak

There is a very involved and intricate system of back roads that would lead the traveller between the villages of Sandhurst and Finchampstead. It is safer to take the Wokingham Road, and then turn left at a roundabout near Crowthorne station. This leads through the famous avenue of sequoias to the even more famous Finchampstead Ridges. Passing this and the war memorial just as one enters the village, make a right turn into Church Lane. The Queen's Oak is to be found at the top of this narrow and twisting lane.

The Queen's Oak (incidentally the only one of this name in the country) is the archetypal English pub, in a near faultless English setting. Long summer evenings in the shadow of the ancient church give an atmosphere of sedate serenity.

There have been rumours of a spiritual customer visiting the pub for years. It is a little old lady who frequents the old saloon bar, now a non-smoking lounge. She has a favourite seat near the bar.

There is no way in which one can look up the pedigree of a spectral visitor. Post offices and libraries do not have reference lists; one chance of obtaining information is to try and glean it from the more elderly residents of the community. This failing, the enquirer has the final option – a seance – and this is exactly what a group of customers did.

Through a ouija board, the small group of rather reticent friends, several of whom were sceptical in the extreme, managed to contact a small boy and his grandmother. Little further information could be gleaned from the child, other than that he had once lived locally – whether actually at the Queen's Oak or merely nearby was not established.

The episode was described as uncanny, the outcome being that those who had arrived with the more cynical attitude had left the most convinced.